The Hart Method

Method

Christine Hart

A 21 Day Guided
Meditation Program

Layover Productions LLC

Daily Meditation Guide

Day One Practice – You are loved

Day Two Practice – You are cherished

Day Three Practice - You are supported

Day Four Practice – You are never alone

Day Five Practice – You are limitless

Day Six Practice – You are a spiritual being

Day Seven Practice – You are valuable

Day Eight Practice – You are brave

Day Nine Practice – You are guided

Day Ten Practice – Your voice matters

Day Eleven Practice – You are magnificent

Day Twelve Practice – You are joy

Day Thirteen Practice – You are a masterpiece

Day Fourteen Practice – You are light

Day Fifteen Practice – You are reborn every day

Day Sixteen Practice – You are eternal

Day Seventeen Practice – You are open

Day Eighteen Practice – You are connected

Day Nineteen Practice - You are a healer

Day Twenty Practice – You are an angel

Day Twenty-One Practice – You are invincible

Congratulations! You have taken the first step in honoring the light in you! You have chosen to commit to 21 days of meditation practice. As you know, it takes 21 days to create a new habit. You have been guided to read this book, and whether you are aware of it or not, you chose this book for a reason. The reason could be that you want a deeper connection to God, the Universe, Source, Divine Mind, or Intelligence. Or the reason could be you are curious about meditation. However, this book came to you, honor it. It was not by chance. You are a spiritual being living a physical life and now you will begin to tap into the essence that is you. Meditation is a beautiful practice that will take you into your inner landscape and help you discover the riches that you have within you. You were born with everything you need in life, you only need to get quiet and allow the stirrings from within to bubble up and guide you. You are about to embark on a journey of a lifetime. The journey within.

What is Meditation?

Meditation is a practice where you place your attention on an object, a word, or a repeated phrase, to keep you focused for a period of time. Meditation has been proven to relieve stress and anxiety and to help us achieve a calm mental state.

There are many kinds of meditation,

there is no wrong way to meditate.

Before we get started, I feel compelled to share with you my journey and my story. The defining moment in my life happened on April 28, 2012. That was the day my whole world crumbled. My husband of 17 years broke down and told me he was having an affair. I felt physically sick and in a state of shock. We did what most people do, we went into therapy. He never ended the affair and I slowly gave up on the dream of repairing the marriage. I began meditating one minute a day. I used the manual, *A Course in Miracles* to guide me. I completely surrendered and trusted that God had a better plan for me. I read and incorporated any techniques that would help me acknowledge and grow through the deep pain I was experiencing. I embraced my faith and let go. I also quit drinking. I wanted total clarity. I felt as though chains and layers of pain were falling off me. I felt like me again. Once I accepted that my husband was not going to change his behavior, I went forward with my divorce with no regrets. I learned to trust my intuition again and I have been living from a state of knowingness ever since. My divorce was a blessing.

Meditation transformed me and opened up a whole new world. When I was in my twenties, I did stand up comedy. I loved the feeling of being on stage. I did it on and off for a few years and then I stopped. I focused on my career as a reading teacher and starting a family. However, there was a voice in my head that was with me every time I drove to and from work, "You should be doing stand up." I ignored it. This time I decided to listen to it. I knew I had to return to comedy and commit to a year of it. I had to honor what I had been suppressing for 15 years. I cannot express to you what a gift it was to give myself permission to follow my heart. I knew that I had to share my comedy with the world. We are here for a purpose and we must share our unique gifts and talents so that we live our best life, and in turn be of service to others. During my year of comedy, I felt compelled to share what I learned from the divorce. I realized I wanted to share more than just my comedy. So, I took a leap of faith and I put together workshops about self-discovery and submitted it to my school district. They were approved and I have been running workshops and speaking for years, reminding people of all ages of their value and their worth. The tools and strategies that I use are embraced by the people who take my workshops or listen to me speak. It is an honor to be able to serve these brave souls who are willing to honor what they were meant to do on earth. I have since made a commitment to dedicate the rest of my life to helping others realize their worth and their sole purpose. Now, I would like to share them with you.

Each day is a gift that is given to us every morning. You are not the same person you were yesterday. The breaking of a new day is a golden opportunity to be the being you were created to be. I invite you to begin your day by taking care of you. Each day I will give you a journal exercise. You can express yourself in any way that feels right to you. You can write, draw, use images, post on social media, or make a voice recording. You are connecting to The Divine. When you meditate you will receive nudges and whisperings and when you express yourself right after meditating, you are tapping into your true essence. Trust what comes up, you didn't make it up.

How Do I Meditate?

This next section is how I start my day. I invite you to read through this section and create your own meditation ritual based on what resonates with you.

What has worked for me is this: the moment I open my eyes, I take three deep, long breaths, pausing at the end of each inhalation for a moment and noticing the pause between each breath. This centers me. I sit up in bed and meditate for 10 to 20 minutes. What does meditation look like? Feel like? For me, I start by gently closing my eyes, softening the muscles of my face, smoothing out my brow, unclenching my jaw, allowing my shoulders to relax and drop from my ears. My hands are on my thighs (thighs can be criss-cross applesauce or straight, if you need to be seated, root down through your feet, do this by firmly putting your feet on the ground) palms up because I love to receive what the universe wants to give me, (if that doesn't feel comfortable to you, you can place your palms down, palm over palm, holding your own hands whatever feels natural and most comfortable for you, it just needs to be symmetrical). Align your spine, it's your lifeline, you want it to be straight, but not rigid. Keep your chin straight, imagine at the center of your head there is a string gently pulling your head up. I focus on my breathing, I think, "breathing in," as I am breathing in and "breathing out," as I breathe out.

Sometimes counting settles my thoughts. At the end of the exhalation I think, "one" and then the next exhalation I think, "two", until I get to 10. If I lose track of counting, I just start all over again.

I feel myself sink into my sits bones (my butt) by putting my attention there and feeling as if there is a weight there. I let my hands get heavier and heavier. Sometimes it's effortless and I drift past my current state of mind to a place where I feel as if I am floating and my hands and feet are buzzing, tingling or numb.

Other times I can't quiet my thoughts and they keep coming and all I can do is my best to let them come and go. I do this by acknowledging the thought and saying in my head, "Thank you for sharing." If that doesn't work, I try to let them float on by. I do this by visualizing the words on clouds, or on leaves drifting down a slow, moving river. Even when I am unable to quiet my mind, I stay with the meditation because any meditation is a good meditation, even when I can barely make it through the allotted time. It takes dedication to sit the whole time. The thing is, taking time for you to be still is a gift.

If sitting makes you bonkers, there are so many other ways to meditate such as folding laundry, washing the dishes, walking in nature, walking the dog, doing yoga, jogging, swimming, painting, drawing, coloring, knitting, drinking a cup of coffee or tea, watching a sunset/sunrise, being by a body of water, watching your baby or your kids sleep. Anything that takes you into the moment and you are lost in the beauty of the moment can be a moment of meditation. It's in the breath. The breath is your guide, allow it to center and calm you. It is always available to you.

Walking meditation is another way to stay present in the moment. Mother Earth grounds us and each time you take a step you can honor her and the present moment at the same time. When you are walking you can use mantras and affirmations to keep you present in the moment. Each time your foot touches the ground, you can say any of the following phrases or make up your own positive one, "Thank you, I love you, I am worthy, I am deserving of love, health, success, I am valuable, I am beautiful, I am calm, I am powerful, I matter." Being in nature and appreciating the beauty of being outside is another form of meditation. Nature inspires us, soothes us, and reminds us that even though we may be in Winter, Spring is coming. Take time to be in nature every day.

That can be your form of meditation. Another form of meditation is taking a hot shower, closing your eyes and allowing yourself to feel the water on your head. Remember, there is no "right" way to meditate, whatever works for you is the right one.

By cultivating a daily meditation practice you are building a foundation that will fortify you for whatever the day holds. You are the most important person in your life. When you honor yourself first, you are recognizing that you are valuable and worthy. When you incorporate meditation into your daily routine it has the potential to change your whole life.

The 21 Days of Self Discovery

This book is designed to take you through 21 days of meditation. The purpose is for you to find what works for you and apply it. I have included tips and strategies that have changed my life and the lives of the people I have worked with. It is my hope and my prayer that you walk away with something of value. Time is precious and I want you to honor your time and dedication. Please be gentle with yourself. Take it moment by moment.

Each day of this program gives you a tool or a technique to focus on for that day. Take only what appeals to you. Every day you will start by doing the morning ritual that is given to you on day one. It will be the same ritual every morning of the program. If you need to refer to the method, simply look back to day one. Eventually you will have it down deep in your being and you will be able to do it automatically.

Day One Practice - You are loved.

Be proud of yourself that you are embarking on a journey that starts with a single step. You are worthy.

Morning Meditation

The following is what I do every morning. You may use this as a guide for you to start your day. Use whatever speaks to you. Refer to it as much as you need to. On each practice day, there will be a daily reminder for you to do your **morning meditation**. I will also include suggestions on each day so you can experience moments of meditation throughout the day. I invite you to create your own. I wanted to give you a glimpse into how I start my day.

Meditation in the morning is how I begin my day. The beginning of the day is sacred time. Set the tone of your day by taking care of you first. When I first began, I started with a minute. I would read from *A Course of Miracles* and then I set the timer on my phone for a minute. I took a couple of deep breaths to slow down my thoughts and to get quiet and centered. Then I would close my eyes and attempt to meditate. At first it was so difficult to sit still, forget about quieting my over-active brain. I just wanted the timer to go off. But, I was determined to create this new habit, and I refused to give up. I was gentle with myself and I committed 100% to cultivating this practice. I took baby steps. Once I could do a minute, I extended the time to a minute and a half. I built up my daily practice slowly. It took me months to get up to 20 minutes a day. Now, I meditate three times a day. I cannot live without it. Meditating has profoundly changed my life. I am more patient, calm, compassionate, open and aware. I truly meet people where they are, everyone has their own struggles and that is what connects us.

Meditation has the potential to profoundly change your life as well. Change is an inside job. Take care of your inner world first. So, please take your time and don't give up! If it is too overwhelming to start with a minute, then start with 30 seconds. The key is to begin! Create an area where you feel comfortable and relaxed. It can be your bedroom, or a special room. Have a cushion or a comfortable chair ready for use. To quiet your mind, pick a word or a mantra to keep you focused. You can even light a candle to focus on. Softly gaze at the flame. (Do that by allowing your eyes to go soft, let your eyes get heavy in the sockets, and allow your lids to close halfway). Make sure the word is a benign word (calm, peace, love, grateful, forgiveness, hope, joy, trust) and the mantra is positive (I am worthy, I am love, I am valuable, I am peace, I am loyal, I matter, I am valuable, I am true) repeat the word or mantra over and over. When thoughts come, and they will, do your best to let them pass you by. Always be gentle with yourself. You are doing the best you can in every moment. Everyone is. Commit to do this practice for 21 days. I encourage you to keep some sort of a record about how you feel after meditation. This will allow you to see your progress over the next three weeks. Whatever impressions that come up during this time, honor them. You did not make them up. Words, feelings, colors, music, animals, insects, flowers, objects, whatever comes up is from The Divine. For the first seven days of meditation you will stick with either a minute of meditation or 30 seconds.

The following are suggestions to help you start your day off right. I do these practices right after my morning meditation.

Three Gratefuls

Research says that if you begin a new practice and do it for 21 days in a row, you have created new neural paths in the brain and a new habit has formed. Every morning after meditation, say what you are grateful for. You can think of them, writing is even more powerful, but if you are pressed for time, think them. Nothing is too small to be grateful for. ("I am grateful for coffee, I am grateful that it's Friday, I am grateful that I know what I am wearing today, I am grateful that I have a job, I am grateful that my cat is next to me, I am grateful that I am alive…")

The Nostril Test

This technique is from Kundalini yoga. You simply take your pointer finger and close your right nostril and breathe in and out and then you close your left nostril with your pointer finger and breathe in and out. Whichever nostril is clearer is the foot you step out of bed with. You are literally starting your day by stepping out on the "right" foot. If both are clear, your choice!

Mirror Work

This is from the late, great Louise Hay. Mirror work is so simple, yet so profound. When you go to the bathroom, look into the mirror, look into your eyes, which are the windows of the soul and say, "I love you, (your name)," and stay with it. If that is too hard, you can say, "I am willingly to love you, (your name)." Get comfortable with being uncomfortable. Looking at ourselves through the lens of love can be difficult. Our brains are trained to look for what is lacking, we need to retrain our brains to look at ourselves the way the Divine would gaze upon us. Look into your beautiful eyes and feel the words, "I love you......." When you dedicate yourself to this practice, you catch glimpses of your radiant beauty. This is not only part of your morning ritual, it is a practice you do throughout the day. Every time you pass a mirror throughout the day, say, "I love you." Your goal is to do it a hundred times a day! This tool alone will create small inner shifts that create big changes. It's a personal favorite.

Practice morning meditation.

Speaking Point- We all express ourselves in different ways. Write, speak or draw the following:

Write/Say/Draw three things that you love about yourself. Read them out loud to yourself three times after you Write/Say/Draw them. This is powerful. You are created by love and you need to remind yourself of that.

Day Two Practice - You are cherished.

Breath is life. Bring awareness to your breath today. There is a breathing technique, by Davidji that takes only 16 seconds. It requires that you take two mindful breaths. You begin by taking a deep breath, following the breath as best you can through your nostrils, down your throat into your chest, down through your abdomen, pause, and observe that breath in your abdomen, then exhale following the breath as best you can back up through your nostrils and observe it going out into air around you. Repeat. For those 16 seconds, you were fully present, not thinking about the past or the future. So, whenever you are feeling overwhelmed, use this technique. And finally do this breathing right before you enter where you live. It will reframe your mindset, and your loved ones will benefit as a result. The breath will bring you into the present.

Check in how you feel immediately after you have done this simple technique. I always feel better.

Practice morning meditation.

You are still in the beginning phase of transformation. It is so important that you go at your own pace. The last 45 minutes before you go to bed is an important time. You are setting yourself up for sleep. The brain remembers most clearly the last 45 minutes before bed. You need to be watching, reading or listening to things that bring calm, peace or uplifting feelings of joy. This is an excellent time to do a guided meditation. Ask for whatever you need, the answer has the potential to come to you in your dreams.

As you go about your day, take the opportunity to take two deep breaths while at a stop light, waiting on line, before answering an email, a text or a phone call. Deep breaths center and calm you. We all have a "pause" button in the center of our forehead. It is called the Bindi spot. It is located between your eyebrows, slightly above where your eyebrows meet. You take your index finger and gently massage that spot in a circular motion. It is also an acupuncture spot. Massage it until you feel a sense of peace. Use this when feeling overwhelmed. It has been known to lessen headache pain. The breath will bring you back into the present moment, and that is all we have.

Speaking Point

Check in with how you are feeling right now. Say it out loud. Now take 3 deep breaths. The biggest breaths you have taken all day. Write/Draw/Speak how you feel now. Any different? The breath is our Spirit. It is always available to us. When we have the awareness to use our breath to calm and center us, we make better choices.

Day Three Practice - You are supported.

Mother Earth grounds us and supports us. She is our foundation and our security. When we are walking mindfully we become aware that we are never alone, our footsteps are being guided. The earth is a reminder that we are not alone. Feel its solid support. We have unwavering guidance and walking meditation reminds us of that. Take time today to do mindful walking meditation. You are sending out a powerful message.

Practice morning meditation.

Pick a mantra or an affirmation today that you can say as you walk. Every time your foot touches the ground you say. "I love you, I am worthy, I am valuable, I am overflowing with abundance, I am responsible, I am creative, I am a masterpiece, I am beautiful, I am smart, I am successful, I am fit and healthy." Or an affirmation, "I am worthy and deserving of great success, I am worthy of great love, I am speaking all over the world, I am receiving accolades for the book I wrote, I am earning extreme wealth through my company, I am in demand and I have offers pouring in, I am living in my luxurious penthouse apartment." This practice keeps you grounded in the moment. I also find myself tuning into my surroundings. I notice what is happening in nature and what is showing up for me to guide me. Animals, insects, flowers, people I pass. Pay attention to what appears wherever you are, especially if it is not something you see, hear, or read every day. The Universe is always communicating with you.

How many times have you thought about someone you haven't seen or heard from in a while and you suddenly receive a text or you just happen to run into that person?

Speaking Point

When did you do your walking meditation?
Write/Draw/Speak the mantra or
affirmation that you used. What did you
see, feel, sense and know?
Write/Draw/Speak your experience.

Day Four Practice - You are never alone.

We have this incredible ability to attract what we want. When we focus on what we want, our whole perspective changes. We see the world as a place of love and belonging.

Practice morning meditation.

Today, be sure to focus your thoughts on only what you want. Don't worry about the how, the how will show up. Get laser focused on what you want. I always include God (Universe, Higher Power, Divine Intelligence, Source) when I am focusing on what I want, I think/say, "This or better." God always has bigger and better plans for us. Why not be bold and ask for the big dream? Simply make your requests and let go. Trust. The Universe is always answering you. Are you receiving what you want? If not, now is the time to take action.

I recommend that you write a "Dear God" (Universe, Higher Power, Divine Intelligence, Source) letter. Get clear on what you want. Write from your heart. There are no limits. Write as if you have access to everything, because you do! Visualize your dream house, partner, car, vacation…. have fun with it! Write in present tense, "I am living my best life. I am writing, speaking and publishing books." Speak it into being. Write as if you are living it, we are always living what we are speaking, thinking, and believing. So start today, reclaim your birthright, your joy, your innate goodness. Be sure to put a date and time on it, that way the Universe knows that you are serious. The more specific, the better.

When you are finished, mail it. That could mean, sticking it in your desk drawer, or putting it in a shoe box, anywhere you like. The point is to release your dreams into the universe and let the law of attraction do its thing. Most importantly, trust. Let go, and surrender. That is where the bliss is. And what happens is simply unbelievable. Here is one of my Dear God letters.

May 5, 2013

Dear God,

Thank you for sending me this wonderful man. He is funny, smart, generous, kind, adventurous, sexy, athletic, sensitive, strong, friendly, hard-working, open and honest. I love how he makes me laugh every day and how caring he is with my kids. I love waking up next to him. He is truly present and the ideal life partner. He believes in me, my goals, and totally supports me in all that I do. He has a heart of gold and he would do anything for me. I love the life that we have together. I see him coming into my life by August 2, 2013 at 3:30 p.m.

Thank you, God, for all the beauty you have brought into my life.

Respectfully and humbly yours,

Christine Hart

On June 9, 2012 I was on my way home from Brooklyn. My first husband had the kids and I called him on the way home to check on them. He wasn't feeling well so I offered to pick them up on my way home. I picked them up early and headed for home. My sister called me and invited us over. I was in no rush to get home. Plus, the kids could hang out with their cousins. When I got there my nephew Scott asked me if I would take all the kids to the park. I agreed to take the boys and the girls would stay at my sister's. The park we went to was not the park we normally go to and my sister, Nancy, was advising me against it due to parking. But, Scott was so earnest about going to that specific park, I said, "Yes." We got there and I found a parking spot easily (a good omen!) I settled myself on an empty bench, opened the book I was reading and lost myself in it. A blonde headed boy caught my attention and I looked as if he wanted to join in with my kids. So, I jumped up, and introduced my kids to him and off they went playing. I went back to my book. I then noticed a guy looking around, I figured the blonde boy was his. I let him know where he was and that he was playing with my kids. Again, I went back to my book. The next thing I know, I am chatting away with this guy and when I found out he was divorced I was so psyched! I could get the male perspective on my situation through objective eyes! I figured I would NEVER see this guy again, I told him things I hadn't told a soul.

I was still holding on to the last shred of hope that I could save my marriage. So, when he said this simple sentence, I was stopped in my tracks. "What makes you think if you took him back this time it would be any different?" That's when it hit me. My husband wasn't going to change his behavior. Suddenly, it was if a veil was lifted and I could see clearly. We chatted a bit more and we even played baseball with his daughter and my son. Then it was time to go. He asked if we could exchange numbers and I said, "Sure," knowing full well that I was NEVER going to text him, after all, I pretty much gave him full disclosure of what was happening in my life! Plus, I had my first Iphone at the time and I wasn't all that great with adding contacts. So, I attempted to put him into my contacts and went to my sister's house. I jokingly told her I met a guy. The next day at work I shared what happened with my inner circle of friends who knew what was going on. They were all over me! "You have to text him!" "No way," was my response. I ended up sending a text to him to thank him. Apparently, I had saved him in my favorites, under "John Park Dad." We started hanging out as friends, and our relationship evolved. John was the man I had written about in my Dear God letter. He leapt off the page and into my heart. We got married on August 14, 2015.

God answered my Dear God letter earlier than expected. I met John on June 9 2013, in the late afternoon. If I had checked the time, I have no doubt it was 3:30. That's the power of Dear God letters.

Speaking Point

Write/ Draw/ Speak your own Dear God letter. Put your heart and soul into it. Go big! Notice how you feel when you "send" it.

Day Five Practice – You are limitless.

A clutter-free dwelling equals a clutter-free mind. When we create a space that is organized and inviting, we change our whole mindset. We free up energy that has become clogged and we liberate our spirit.

Practice morning meditation.

There is this great book, *The Joy of Tidying Up*, by Marie Kondo. I recommend that you purchase it. I love this book! The tip about how to fold your clothes alone is worth it. I used to fold and put my clothes away in a drawer and not think much of it. Well, let me tell you, Marie's tip on how to fold your shirts, sweaters, socks, pants, etc. is eye-opening. Fold them like rectangles and lay them on their side, instead of on top of each other. You open the drawer and they are lined up on their side, you can see all of your clothes! Everything is side by side! No more lifting and searching, you open a drawer and you can see everything! It is magic! This simple tip alone lightens you up. We only have so much energy in the day and dealing with mess and items that no longer serve us is a tremendous energy suck. Look around your house and make a list of what needs to be thrown out, fixed, or donated. Also, see who you can delegate certain chores to do and more importantly by when. By putting a specific date and time you are acknowledging the importance of getting the task done. Checking items off this list as simple as it sounds creates shifts. You will feel like a weight has been lifted. You will feel lighter and you will most likely stand a little bit taller.

Speaking Point

Write/ Speak/ Draw what your ideal home would look like. Where would it be? What kind of home would it be? How would it feel when you enter it? How would you decorate it?

Day Six Practice - You are a spiritual being.

Be gentle with yourself. When you make a mistake that hurts yourself or others it's your humanness coming through. Remember we are spiritual beings living a physical life.

All hurt matters, big and small. The body remembers all hurts, which is why it is so important to check in with the body during meditation. When our emotional pain becomes blocked energy in the body, we have the opportunity to release it. We need to do a body scan and we need to identify where the pain is and honor it.

Practice morning meditation.

The Sedona method is just one way to do this. I invite you to do this scan before bed. I invite you to sink into your bed and get comfortable. Close your eyes and take three to five deep breaths to calm and center you. Make sure you are on your back and your hands are at your sides, palms up or palms down. Now, I want you to envision, as best you can, a scanner, the size of a rectangle that can encompass your front and back body. This scanner is white and we will start at the top of the head and slowly scan the front and back of the body. Go at your own pace. Once you have identified a part of the body that is in pain, stay there. Welcome the pain, as best you can. Experience the sensations, as best you can. Thank it for showing up. If it feels comfortable for you put your hand on the area. Massage the area. Ask it questions, "What do I need to do to release this pain?" Listen.

Honor whatever comes up. When you feel ready, ask, Could I let this pain go? If the answer is yes, then ask yourself, Would I let this pain go? If the answer is yes, then ask, When? If the answer is now, then let it go. If the answer is no, ask yourself, after I have a conversation with (mom, dad, sibling, aunt, uncle, boss, friend, cousin…..) And if the answer is still no, that's okay. You have honored your pain by acknowledging it and that is a step in the right direction. After you have done one scan of the body and you feel up to it, I invite you to do another one. This is a powerful practice and I applaud you for being brave. We humans tend to run away, ignore, shop, eat, smoke, vacation or drink our pain away. This will release even more blocks and you may experience shifts in your inner world.

Speaking Point

**Write/ Draw/ Speak about the Sedona
Method. How did you feel after this
experience? Is it a method you would
incorporate into your meditation practice?**

Day Seven Practice - You are valuable.

Do something for you today. You are the most important person in your life. When you take care of you, you are elevating your vibrational level.

Practice morning meditation.

There are so many ways to honor you. What have you been putting off that you would really like to do? From a simple cup of tea with a dear friend, to a massage, walking in nature, shopping, baking, organizing, whatever makes your heart sing is what you do today. Make **YOU** the priority. You deserve it! Be proud of yourself, you have been meditating for seven days in a row! You are well on your way to making meditation a daily practice!

Speaking Point

Write/ Draw/ Speak what did you do for you today? How did you feel about making you the priority? Every day is a golden opportunity to put you first. Once you take of you first, you're able to serve others better. You are number one.

Great job! You have just completed seven days of your meditation practice. Be proud of yourself that you have completed the first week of your three week commitment. Check in with yourself, how are you feeling? This week you are looking to increase your time. Depending on where you started on day one, extend your meditation for 30 seconds or a minute.

Day Eight Practice - You are brave.

You have all that you need to take a risk. You do not need to do one thing more. You are ready. Pick an area of your life that you would like to focus on. It could be health, a relationship, career, financial, spiritual, community, or recreational. Make it a priority to commit to doing a small goal towards achieving what you would like to accomplish. I say small because we tend to put so much pressure on ourselves to perform at a level that we have trouble maintaining and then we overwhelm ourselves and give up. What can you do today that you know you will be able to do by bedtime. It can be as simple as making a phone call, taking a walk, writing for ten minutes, clearing out one drawer, signing up for a class, contacting an organization that you have always wanted to contribute to. Once you have honored your goal, you have caused an inner shift and that's where the magic is. Small shifts equal big changes.

Practice morning meditation.

It's important to get out of your comfort zone. We are creatures who prefer to be comfortable. It is vital that you take a healthy risk and take a leap of faith. What have you been ignoring? What has your heart been whispering or shouting at you to pay attention to? Honor your heart's wisdom, don't wait a second longer. When the idea or urge hits, jump on it! The universe loves to honor boldness. Make that phone call, start that book, start that blog, end that relationship, go to the gym, put down that fork, you know what it is.

The time is now. The very act of taking that first step increases energy and lightness to your being. When you honor your heart's desire, you are liberated.

Speaking Point

Write/ Draw/ Speak how did it feel to commit to doing something that you really wanted to do?

Day Nine Practice - You are guided.

Coincidences are God's way of remaining anonymous. Synchronicity is one way God (Universe, Higher Power, Divine Intelligence, Source) communicates with us. Once you are awake and aware, you are more intuitive. You trust the signs and the opportunities that are being presented to you. You are attuned to the magic of the universe and miracles enfold all around you because you believe. God is always communicating with you. You only need to trust and let go.

Practice morning meditation.

Are we listening and paying attention? When you notice patterns and things that keep showing up, honor them. This is synchronicity. Signs come in so many forms. Nature, animals, insects, license plates, songs, conversations, angel cards, colors, numbers, and books are just a few of the ways God (Universe, Divine Mind, Source, Intelligence) is trying to communicate with us. They are meant to guide us. Are we awake and aware of the guidance that is always available to us? In your meditation today, ask for a sign. Honor whatever comes up, you did not make it up. Be on the look-out today for signs, it's incredible how they show up.

I have been guided by all of the methods mentioned above.

One of the most profound signs I received was when I was struggling with the decision to get divorced. I felt so alone and lost and I didn't know what to do anymore. I wanted to do what was right for me and my kids. I was desperate for a sign. I have always believed in God and I got down on my knees and asked, "Am I making the right decision to get divorced?" I had been wrestling with that decision and I was at my lowest point. I drove to work that day and on the way home I was thinking about what I should do, and at a stop light, I saw in front of me a blue jeep that had a license plate that read, "DNTGIVUP". I knew immediately that was my sign, Don't Give Up. I felt heard and empowered that I was doing the right thing and a weight lifted. Anytime I faltered, I would see a license plate that would let me know that I was doing the right thing. I would see;

ANGELS, BLESSED, DIVNMIND, WATTNXT,

GRACENOW, MAKEITSO, MENT2BE, those are just a few! To this day I am still being guided by license plates.

Speaking Point

Write/ Draw/ Speak what you noticed today, google spiritual meaning of whatever it was that you noticed. Read until something makes sense to you. For example, red robins represent transformation and change.

Day Ten Practice - Your voice matters.

Your voice needs to be counted and heard. Speak your truth. Speak in the way that is most natural to you. You may be a writer, speaker, singer, dancer, listener, athlete, scholar, nature lover, animal lover, computer guru, musician, poet, scuba diver, artist, whatever your talent, that is your voice.

Practice morning meditation.

When we were kids we naturally lived out loud. We cried when we were hungry or hurt, we laughed and saw the beauty that is life. We lived in the now. We spoke our truths and loved openly. As we got older we felt the need to please our parents, grandparents, teachers, coaches, aunts and uncles, to name a few. We silenced our voices to appear polite, and appropriate. We stopped honoring the unique individual that God created us to be. Today make it a point to live out loud. If you can, go outside and listen to the birds sing. Let them inspire you to speak your truth, to be seen and heard. Your presence is needed and necessary on this earth.

Speaking my truth has liberated me from shame and guilt. When I finally opened up to my family and my inner circle of friends about what was going on in my marriage, I felt a tremendous sense of relief. Shame can only thrive in darkness, and when I brought it out into the light, it disappeared. Shame cannot live in the light. We are all connected. It is through our innate compassion that we have for one another that allows us to heal.

Our hearts naturally vibrate loving energy, especially when a loved one is in pain.

I am extremely grateful that I finally allowed myself to share my pain, it saved my life. I got me back, and at the time, I didn't even know I was lost. If you are ever in a place where you feel so ashamed, please turn to a trusted loved one, one who is an exceptional listener, they are the empathetic people who will listen with their whole being. Unloading your burden will allow you to find your voice again. And then, you can sing, loud and proud and be the beautiful spiritual being that you are.

Speaking Point

Write/ Draw/ Speak something you have been ashamed about. Now answer yourself as your best friend would answer you. Feel the love and acceptance flood your being.

Day Eleven - You are magnificent.

You were created by love to love. That is our purpose to love one another.

Practice morning meditation.

The world would only have you focus on what is "wrong" with you. There is so much more "right" with you. Turn off the news, and ignore social media. Take a moment and ask yourself, "Do I own my electronics or do they own me?" Stand out from the crowd. What are your strengths and gifts? Tap into them. What comes easy to you does not come easy to another person and we need to be reminded of that. Our gifts and strengths are what we need to cultivate and then share them with the world. What can you share today? Your beautiful smile is one of the best things to share.

I used to drive to work every day with the voice in my head saying, "You should be doing stand-up." Over and over the whole way in. Once I got to work, the voice stopped. When I left the building, there it was again the whole way home, "You should be doing stand up." I ignored it. I thought that eventually it would go away. It didn't.

In October of 2013 I started going for reiki (energy healing) and I began to remember my dreams again. I would share these dreams with my reiki healer and she would interpret them with me. Then I had the most vivid dream I ever had in my life. This dream was unlike any other I had ever had. It was in black and white and I was rushing through a forest where I kept encountering obstacles, and I felt a sense of urgency. The path was rocky and I had to watch out for roots that were trying to trip me up. I had an appointment and I didn't want to be late. There was a feeling of dread in the forest and I wanted to get out. All of sudden, I broke out and everything was in technicolor, like in the Wizard of Oz. It was a gorgeous day, the sky a color of blue that I can't describe, and I was on the whitest, most pristine beach. Everything about this dream was otherworldly. I was rushing to make my appointment and I found myself passing the most gorgeous man I had ever seen in my life. I almost passed him by because I was so focused on making my appointment.

I felt drawn to him, he was wearing the whitest robe I had ever seen, and running down the sides of it were magnificent jewels, again I have no words that would do these brilliant jewels justice. He gave me the most beautiful smile, he had dark wavy hair, dark eyes and his whole being radiated joy at seeing me. He said to me, "You are 15 minutes late." He was funny and we were laughing and kidding around. I asked him, "Am I doing the right thing?" And just like that, the dream ended. I woke up and the energy in the room was palpable, I knew in my deepest core, that was not just a dream.

When I shared the "dream" with my reiki healer, she said that I had met my spiritual guide. Her question to me was, "What were you doing 15 years ago?" The answer, stand up comedy. The minutes represented years. I decided right there and then that I would commit to a year of comedy. And that is exactly what I did. I did the open-mic circuit, and I even got paid once! That makes me a professional, by the way! Towards the end of my commitment, I realized that I wanted more than to just make people laugh, I wanted a deeper connection with my audience. I wanted to use my experiences and my struggles to help others realize their true value and worth. My year of comedy was a gift, it silenced the voice in my head and I realized my true calling, to use my humor to uplift and inspire others to realize their true worth and purpose.

Speaking Point

Write / Draw/ Speak what have you been ignoring that you know that you were born to do? What can you do today to move in the direction of your dreams? Do it. No step is too small.

Day Twelve -You are joy.

Spread your joy through hugs. It's simple and it's free.

Practice morning meditation.

Oxytocin, calms your nervous system and boosts positive emotions. One of the best ways of releasing this feel- good chemical is through a hug. Hugs say, "I am here for you, I love you, I support you." When we hug, it lowers our blood pressure and it is especially helpful when we are feeling anxious. It also lowers cortisol, which is a stress hormone. Hugs last an average of three seconds, and their effects are immediate. It also puts us in the present moment. Being in the "now" is all we have. Research says, we need four hugs a day to survive, eight to maintain, and twelve to thrive. Make it a point today to give/receive twelve hugs. And pet hugs count!

I am a hugger. When I read that research it reaffirmed for me the power of touch. I am a high school teacher and I am always offering hugs. As my students enter and leave my room we are hugging each other. The heart to heart hug is the most natural. That is when you are embracing in a knowingness that you are safe. It's not too tight, it's not too long, there is no patting of the back. You are in the moment. That simple act fortifies and nourishes your soul. Hug often. Be sure to ask first! Some of my students prefer a fist bump.

Speaking Point

Write/ Draw/ Speak how did this experience feel? Did you find yourself feeling differently after hugging?

Day Thirteen - You are a masterpiece.

Thoughts become things. Think good thoughts.

Practice morning meditation.

We think 60,000 to 80,000 thoughts a day. Over half are negative. It is imperative that we think good thoughts. When a negative thought pops up, immediately say to yourself, "Thank you for sharing." Immediately say a positive thought to replace the negative. We need to get rid of the negative recordings that play over and over in our head. They have been there for years, be vigilant. You have the power to change your thought life. You will in time be able to quiet the inner critic. By saying thank you to it, you are acknowledging it and moving on. This practice will cause inner shifts and you will stand taller and have more confidence because you will be focusing on your innate goodness.

It is almost incredible how much our thought life affects our external life. When we are feeling on top of the world, like when we fall in love, we see the world as the most wonderful place. We are smiling and happy and the world is our oyster. We see solutions, we are living our best self. When we are in struggle we need to have practices in place that will pull us out of the doldrums. One of the best ways is to be extremely aware of our thoughts. Only think good thoughts. Thoughts become things. Thoughts are energy.

What are you sending out? When you think a negative thought about someone-BAM it's out in the energy waves and it is affecting that person. Only wish them love and light. You will feel better. We create these neural clusters around everyone in our lives. Spouses, kids, friends, co-workers, bosses, in-laws,etc. become aware of what you are thinking about when the people in your world pop in your mind. First step is awareness, the second step is to change/substitute the negative thought. Simply send them a great day and success. It's for you as well as for them. You aren't wasting your time thinking a bad thought, which sucks your energy. You are sending positivity out into the universe and that uplifts your energy. We only have so much energy in the day, don't let your thought life take your energy. Use your thought life to uplift you and others!

Speaking Point

Write/ Draw/ Speak when you were aware of your negative thoughts today. Did you remember to say, "Thank you for sharing?" Paying attention to our thought life is a lifelong journey. Be vigilant, you are worth it. Thoughts become things!

Day Fourteen - You are light.

Use your sense of humor to keep heavy situations light. Laugh at the absurdity of life.

Practice morning meditation.

Laughter is a powerful endorphin release. You lose so much through laughter, you lose: anger, stress, sadness, frustration, to name a few. Make it an intention to up your laugh quota today. You will be surprised at what situations present themselves so you can laugh. Laughter unites us and connects us. We experience oneness. Look for the humor in all situations and you will change the energy in the space you are in. Laughter is contagious and the vibe in the area you are in will go up. You will be filled with light and love as a result of a good laugh.

Speaking Point

Write/ Draw/ Speak what situation were you able to use humor instead of frustration, anger, or disappointment? One of the best ways to use humor is when something breaks or spills.

Today is the beginning of the last seven day cycle in your meditation practice, you are making yourself a priority and you need to honor that! Take a moment to look back over the last 14 days and be proud of your commitment to creating a new habit.

Day Fifteen - You are reborn every day.

You have qualities that make you stand out in the crowd. Your smile, your eyes, your innate beauty shines through.

Practice morning meditation.

Happy Birthday! Every day is your "birth" day as each day is a gift. We never know when our last day will be. Today, spend it as if it is your last day. Forgive, say, "I love you," "I am proud of you," "I am so thankful that you are in my life." Hug your loved ones and breath in that sacred moment of heart to heart connection. We tend to fall into the "doing" of life, our days melt into the same routines and responsibilities. Remember you are a spiritual being. How are you "being?" Make today count. Play hooky, cook your family's favorite meal, or go out to dinner. Be present in every interaction you have today and make it a point to leave the other person smiling. Then, you will have spent this day, this one day, in a beautiful way.

Speaking Point

Write/ Draw/ Speak how did you spend this day? What stands out for you?

Day Sixteen - You are eternal.

Your impact is everlasting. The smallest acts of kindness make huge differences. The ripple effect of these acts spread far and wide. When you smile at a stranger, you uplift them as well as yourself. Make your child's bed today, leave a sticky note on the bathroom mirror that says, "You are beautiful." Surprise your partner or spouse with a lunch or dinner date. Pick up the dry cleaning. Book a weekend away. Pick up your kid's favorite ice cream. Write a letter of appreciation to a loved one and mail it.

Practice morning meditation.

Take your time today. Take time to focus on one thing at a time. When you are driving, notice what you are passing by. Your familiar route may surprise you. The leaves may be changing, there may be a license plate in front of you that is meaningful to you, or a spirit animal may show up. When you interact with others, slow down. You have all the time you need. I love to buy strangers coffee. I leave for work early and when I stop at my local deli, I randomly buy coffee for the next person. I feel so good leaving knowing I am surprising someone with a cup of joe. It doesn't cost a lot and it brightens someone else's day. I know, because when I went in recently for my cup of joe, it was on the house!

Speaking Point

Write/ Draw/ Speak what showed up for you today? How was it meaningful for you?

Day Seventeen - You are open.

Make today a yes day. Say yes to you, your kids, your partner and you will have a day filled with surprises. Buy that jacket, shoes, book that vacation, or go to dinner with friends. Say yes to something you might normally say no to you. You are letting the universe know that you are ready for adventure and who knows where a yes could lead you. Trust the opportunities that come up, no matter how small they may seem. Don't wait to be ready to say yes, you are ready! You will have the energy. Saying yes to you and to your loved ones increases your energy.

Practice morning meditation.

I did this with my son, Finn, over the summer. He came up to me in the kitchen with his friend Connor standing beside him. "Ma, can I ask you something?" "The answer is yes, whatever you are asking me, the answer is yes." His eyes got BIG. "Really?" "Yep." "So, Connor can sleep over?" (I am not a fan of sleep overs.) "Yes." Finn gave me a big hug and they raced out to let Connor's mom know. A small request, but it made their day and night!

Speaking Point

**Write/ Draw/ Speak who did you surprise
with a yes answer? Was it you?**

Day Eighteen - You are connected.

See yourself in others. When we do that, we are able to see with our hearts. Then all we will see is how we are connected.

Practice morning meditation.

We are all fractured souls. Somewhere along the line we lost trust in ourselves. We did this by saying we would do something for ourselves and we didn't follow through with the promises we made. This affects us, whether we are cognizant of it or not. These broken promises compromise our self-worth and esteem. One way to restore our trust in ourselves is to stargaze.

When we take the time to look up into the heavens we are reminded that we are part of its vastness and that we are all connected. We are so much more than what we believe. We have stardust flowing in our veins. Make a commitment to stargaze three to four times a week and you will experience a feeling of peace and oneness.

It sounds so simple, yet it is transformative. Taking ten to fifteen minutes to stargaze is life affirming. We so rarely look to the heavens. We are a part of so much more than this physical plane. Breathe in the night air and listen to the night sounds. Breathe in the expansiveness of the universe. You might even see a shooting star. The night sky is always changing, take the time to look up.

Speaking Point

Write/ Draw/ Speak about your experience stargazing. How did it feel to gaze up at the heavens?

Day Nineteen - You are a healer.

We are all healers. When we give ourselves over in conversation and feel what the other is feeling we are able to let our compassion flow from our core to theirs. Lead with love and compassion.

Practice morning meditation.

Listen more than you speak today. When in conversation listen with your whole body. Listen with your heart and soul. Ask for guidance before you engage. "Please give me the patience to listen without feeling the need to correct, fix, or jump in with my own baggage." "Give me the ability to hear what they are really saying and to honor them by giving them what they need." Being a good listener requires just that, listen. Most of the time that's all anyone needs to figure out what to do next. We just want to be seen and heard. That's why we have two ears and one mouth!

I have the privilege of working with young people and I am honored when they speak with me about what they are struggling with. I pray for guidance right before they share with me and then I listen without judgement. I listen with my heart. I have earned their trust by honoring their truths. They continue to teach me.

Speaking Point

Write/ Draw/ Speak about listening. When you rearrange the letters in listen it spells silent. Were you able to be silent while you were listening? How did that feel?

Day Twenty - You are an angel.

When we have days when we are feeling less then, it is the perfect opportunity to be of service. Be an earth angel today. Do your best to behave like an angel. When you are walking today, say to yourself, "I am an angel." This will remind you to be patient and loving in your interactions today. Hold the door for people, let people go ahead of you, smile at all who pass you.

Practice morning meditation.

When you are feeling down, be of service to someone else. It will lift the person up as well as yourself. It can be as simple as giving a heartfelt compliment, allowing someone to go ahead of you on line, carrying out groceries, or smiling at a stranger. When we go outside of ourselves and help others, we forget our troubles and realize how good we really have it. This gives us a chance to reset ourselves and look at ourselves and others through a lens of compassion.

What helps me is changing my scenery. Taking a drive along the shore, hanging out with people who make me laugh, petting my pets or simply taking a walk. Use technology, YouTube puppies, babies, or kittens. The key is to act fast. Don't wallow. The brain is trained to look for lack and scarcity. Be proactive. Exercising is always the way to go, we always feel so good when we are done!

Speaking Point

Write/ Draw/ Speak how did it feel to be an angel today? What surprised you?

Day Twenty One - You are invincible!

You are limitless. You can do whatever you put your mind to. You are unstoppable. You are never too old or too young.

Practice morning meditation.

Louise Hay published her first book, Heal Your Body, at age 50. Louise went on to have incredible success as a speaker and a writer up until the time of her passing on August 30, 2017. She was 90 years young. Justin Bieber was a singing sensation on YouTube at the age of 12. Although Justin has gone through his share of struggles, his talent has staying power. Age is literally just a number. When an idea strikes, act on it. You will have what you need to move forward when you need it. Remember, the how will show up. When you are inspired, honor it. Your soul is counting on you. We are given a certain number of breaths to breathe. Make every breath count. Seize the day. There is magic in the beginning and there is joy when we finish. Remember, you are powerful.

Speaking Point

Write/ Draw/ Speak what are you ready to commit too? Now is the time. You are enough, you've always been enough. Take that first step!

Celebrate!

You did it! You created a new habit! You stayed the course and you fulfilled your commitment to yourself. Check in with how you feel. Smile and know that you created inner shifts that will equal changes in your outer world. You got out of your comfort zone and did something that was uncomfortable and different. It takes courage to live outside your comfort zone and you did it! You embraced your inner light and as a result, you shine brighter. If you decided to journal, look back from the beginning and see how you have grown. Notice the method you chose to express yourself. Your wisdom is there. What will you use going forward to keep you in the moment?

I encourage you to continue your meditation journey and continue to slowly build up your practice. Make it a goal to meditate 20 minutes a day. Remember to be gentle and to go slowly. It can take months to build up to 20 minutes, so please continue to go at your own pace. Baby steps! You will be a blessing to all of those in your life because of this beautiful practice.

I would love to hear any comments that you would like to share with me. You can reach out to me:

Facebook page: Christine Gorman Hart

YouTube channel: Christine Hart

Instagram: @officialchart

mindfulhart14@gmail.com

Breathe,

Chris Hart 🤍